Urban Inspiration

Inspirational Poetry by:

William H. Stokes

Published by:

THINGS THAT MATTER LLC
GREENSBORO, NC
ISBN: 978-0-692-85979-7

Dedication

This book is dedicated to my Aunt and fellow Poet Rosa Bogar. She authored the first poetry that I put my hands on; "Black Woman Sorrow." Throughout my childhood and even now I have been captivated and inspired by her uniqueness. She dedicates her life to her dreams and fulfilling her purpose. Even though she is still with us; she has already left a legacy. Rosa Bogar is the true definition of a "Living Legend." Her collection "Rosa" reveals the simplicity and complexity of life so eloquently. I have witnessed her work diligently and tirelessly pursuing her passion and her high call in life. Rosa Bogar's life inspires me to stand up; to be bold, to be different and to embrace who I am. Through these words I give a rose; dedicated to my Aunt Rose (Rosa Bogar)

TABLE OF CONTENTS:

The Call

I fell deep in a zone while in prayer at home.
That's when an angel came and handed me a
microphone; and then he said :

"Shalom, I'm giving you peace; even if they don't
nod their heads or move their feet. The words
you speak are more than rhymes to a beat. They
are messages from The Most High; so rather
unique. Don't sweat the techniques of the savage
and beast. Follow The Spirit's lead. Stay on point
and sharp like a crease.

Press through the hard times like a good soldier,
and if you get empty God will fill you up like
Folger's. He'll make you good to the last drop; so
keeping pushing your pen and His Word until
your casket drops; or until Christ comes back
and takes us to the spot. Don't be surprised if
you see Biggie or Pac; but don't be surprised if
not. We all have to go before that Great Throne.
Some might not make it to that Heavenly Home.

Trust & believe... God is heart-broken; but He can't lie so He has to go with what was spoken, and what is written. Not just bits and pieces but every sentence. So if there's no repentance then good riddance.

Spread the message of hope & grace. Tell the sinner that Jesus Christ died in their place. Now they can have abundant life, and everyday is another chance to get it right. It would be a disgrace if they dissed grace; then got cast away once they saw The Father face to face. Treated like a wicked servant because unknowingly but willingly bowed down to idol worship.

Once the angel shuts the gate, and they retire to a fiery grave. It ain't no coming back from eternity. You can't buy your way out; so what good is your currency? Go preach The Gospel with urgency. This is a 911 call. It's an emergency!!

Christ vs. Hip-Hop

It's either altar calls or yes,yes y'all.
Christ on the cross or Pac & Biggie
Smalls. Sermons from the pulpit or fire
bar spitters. Communion bread & wine
or blunts & hard liquor. Choirs in their
robes sing songs from hymn books; while
my mind is consumed with metaphors &
hooks. Rhymes about half-way crooks
being shook walking around with their
heads down. Scared to look.

Preachers speak truth from out the
Good Book, the Prophet speaks words
that they heard from God, but it's
something about Hip-Hop that captures
the heart. It's the swag, the flow, the hi's
and lows. It's like a stronghold to the
soul. I love Christ, but I love Hip-hop
too. So tell me what, the what am I
supposed to do?

These two things are tugging on the strings of my heart; and I really don't want to keep the two apart.

The struggle is real. I don't think you would understand what I'd feel. It's like a soldier with no weapon trapped on a battlefield. With no sword or shield; I'll probably get killed. So The Lord gave a way of escape. Allowed me to love Hip-hop and keep my faith.

So when I say: "Here we go, holla if you hear me yo." Don't get confused just feel my flow, and just know; I'm giving God the glory and won't stop... This is worship. Not Christ vs. Hip-hop.

Get Your Mind Right!!

What if I was consumed with how The Gospel can bring me money? Desiring the cow and bee-hive; instead of milk and honey? Can such selfish thoughts run through my head; like getting a younger chick if my wife were dead? How I can hook up a sermon to have people deceived; twist The Scriptures to have a multitude following me? Make them believe Christ ain't coming back no time soon. You can live how you want. You can sin all day. He already died for your sins the debt is already paid..

You can get drunk, get high, be homosexual. Believe in other gods and be an intellectual. There's no need to pray. It's not effectual. You don't need the Holy Spirit as The One directing you. Believe in who?... Buddha, Krishna, Zeus, Allah?... Nah. If I did that I would be like The Devil; a liar. Instead I put my faith in Jesus Christ and lift Him higher. It grieves me that some will be cast into a lake of fire. Weeping and gnashing of teeth due to unbelief.

My heart cries if just one soul is loss because they continually denied the work of The Cross. There is a Heaven and there is a Hell. The latter is not where God intended any man to dwell. The Devil knows he only has a short time; so until death his goal is to keep people deceived and blind. Get your mind right!!

Whose Life Is It?

My life, my life: the pain, and strife. The grit & grime. The mud & slime. Now transformed into a glorious shine since The Holy Ghost renewed my mind. My eyes have been opened and I can clearly see when I'm on my grind. No, I mean His grind, His time, His shine. Everything I possess is not mine. I received all through Him. God's mercy and grace. I found my life when I laid it down and started seeking His face. Discovered I was hidden in Christ... A Secret Place

Relying on His stamina in this race called life. Once I took a taste; I knew that The Lord is good. He took a little black boy out of the hood. Told him something absurd. He said: "Eat this Word. Then go spit it out on the blocks in the hoods and suburbs. From bankers, lawyers, doctors to the hustlers on the curb. Tell them about The Rock that you serve. That Blood Work. Christ shed it all on The Cross, and The Blood still works."

The Word still works if you work it. Always relying on God's grace at times is a sign of dead faith. That type of faith is worthless. The Holy Spirit leads and guides us. He teaches all; so who is the blame if you continue to fall? Especially if you have been taught, and you received the revelation you've already been purchased for a price... The Ultimate Cost. Why do we continue to crucify Our Savior on The Cross? Whose life is it anyway?

What is Faith?

What is faith? Is it to cease seeking? Believing that you have reached a point of understanding? Is it standing firm on a belief that you question? Unwilling to change direction for fear that your faith will be lost? Are you afraid to pick up your cross?

Whose faith do you follow? Are you in a state of self-denial or soul survival? Did you know that death to the flesh brings forth revival? To the faith-full not the faith-empty. In simplicity. Simply believe seems complex indeed; unless your mind has been freed by the bleed. Yes. The Blood still flows. Jesus is alive and well because He arose.

Amazing how hands with holes can still hold all power. Rain down Living Water that produce inward showers. Purging and purifying. Cleansing and clarifying. Verily,verifying Who He is, was and will be forever more. The One who sits at the right hand of The Father interceding for the saints.

Need faith? It is written. He is The Author. The ink of His pen is Blood and Water. The heart is His tablet. He is The Holy Scribe. His manuscripts are Spirit and Life. Would have died twice for the sake of His bride. Only once was required. He is The Ultimate Sacrifice. What's faith? Believing your beliefs and doubting your doubts. Aligning your heart with what you confess with your mouth. What is your faith?

Just A Man

Everyday it's a struggle just to stay on course. A few of my best friends are now facing divorce. People steady asking me for more and more. The girls in my neighborhood dressing more like whores. My wife is on bed rest so ain't no intercourse. Twins on the way after 7 miscarriages. I feel so burdened down Lord. What man can carry this?

Go to work everyday with a smile on my face. They have no idea how bad I want to leave this place. They don't know I want to walk out and quit today, and feel like I threw years of my life away.

That's why I call on Jesus before my feet hit the floor, and look up to the sky as I walk out my door. My hopes and dreams don't seem like they are coming to pass, and the devil trying to bring up things from my past. I'm not sure how much longer I can last.

My Bible told me I should pray and fast, but when I do; It don't seem like The Lord is moving too fast. I believe that He's working on my behalf, but sometimes it's a struggle to hold on to His hand. Does He understand I'm just a man?

Pain Reliever

Some were searching for truth and when they found it were hurt. That's the reason some stopped going to church. They were being deceived for so long. Traditions had them looking at faith all wrong. Making attempts to stand strong and be pleasing to God; just to find out it was all a facade.

The Holy Spirit exposed impurities and selfish ambitions. On a path to destruction even though there were good intentions. Unwise decisions. Quenching the Holy Spirit. Acting like they didn't hear it. When He speaks; saying the same thing for weeks, months and sometimes even years. Many didn't listen because it didn't tickle the ears.

Tell me something good. Tell me something sweet. Like I'm getting a financial breakthrough next week. I'll jump out my seat and shout about that. Or maybe I'm getting a new car. I would really like that.

It's frustrating to see the trickery of the enemy. Yeah, He's pretty clever. However, if we examined the Scriptures we would know better. So to the chosen ones... Stand your ground. Prophesy against these clowns. Preaching all about money, houses and cars. Acting like Gospel superstars.

Woe unto you. Destruction is near, but if they repent now then there is nothing to fear.

These words are exhortations. Promoting healing for the nation. Receive these words and they will bring forth life. I know it's rough like sand paper and cuts like a knife. But this is a spiritual cutting away and surgical procedure. After the disease is removed, God will apply the Pain Reliever.

Reppin'

I rep Christ like the mayor, councilman or the chair. The government is on His shoulders and He holds it like boulders. Anointed like Folger's - Good to the last drop, but still growing in the faith like cash crops. Keep me out your fields; I'll burn it down. Christ makes me just that hot.

Spit flames to make you switch lanes. No word games, but I flipped the King James.
Now it's the S.IV. - Street International Version. Dr. Kervorkian; call me the spiritual surgeon. Put the sword to the flesh to put the old man to death.

Some say it's hard but it's fair. Weathering the storm, speaking the Word to change the atmosphere. Spit Christ like minute rice or instant grits. At the table I sit. In the presence of my enemies enjoying a feast. Divine Wine and choice meats. Highly seasoned vet; taste the grace in my speech. Rightly divide The Word so I'm able to teach.

Apostolic flow sent to reach lost souls. Stay on my toes and keep watch for the fold. They scattered abroad so that's where I gotta go. Keep it moving because the end is near. Work out my soul salvation with trembling and fear. So I stand for the Gospel in spite of it all. Too many souls may be lost if I drop the ball. So I preach Christ on the streets. Preach Christ with my pen. Compelling all men to repent of their sin.

Some say the church is a joke, and Christ is a hoax. They turned from the faith because of their kinfolk. They've been "church hurt." So we have to preach Christ. No gimmicks or scams. Just preach Christ. No false prophecies. Just preach Christ. Before the laying on of hands; just preach Christ. He's the Way, the Truth and He is The Life. There is power in the name of Jesus Christ. There is healing in the name of Jesus Christ. There is freedom in the name of Jesus Christ. So I lay down my life for the cause of Jesus Christ. I'm Reppin'

Are You Woke??

A fearful slave in the land of the free and the brave. A bird sings hoping to be freed from his cage. Many travel down Broadway, streets of rage. Where death doesn't discriminate by sex, or race. Thank God the sinner's wage was already paid when Christ worked for three days and received a raise. His clothes were left in the grave when the stone was rolled away, but many still don't believe to this very day.

This wicked generation seeks wonders and signs, but why give sight to those who remain spiritually blind? Can darkness shine? Will words of wisdom part from the lips of a fool? Will a wise builder show up to a job with no tools?
Don't be confused. God can transform your life-form in the midst of a storm.

Even though you've been bruised, been shattered
and torn. Jesus Christ was crucified, beaten,
battered and scorned. So you can be reconciled
to The Father; justified and reborn.

The One in the valley is not like White Lilly flour,
because when He arose; He arose with all power.
It wasn't a Big Bang or a meteor shower.
Everything was created by Him. He was there
before God said "Let Us" begin. He didn't say:
what, where, why, when or even how. He
understood that God's Word is now because He is
I AM.

Do you understand what The Spirit just spoke?
He just gave you hope to the ones that are
spiritual broke. Are you woke?

Look Up

She stands on a street corner waiting for someone to love. She looks left, right, looks down but refuses to look above.

You see she's furious with God because He took the best thing she ever had. Her poor, innocent child was murdered by her own dad. What's sad is that he was also the father of her son. He would come home drunk and use her to have a little fun. Her mother wanted to speak up but was afraid. Without her husband; she didn't know how the bills would get paid.

So at an early age, she learned to play the game. Get them before they get you. If they give you one then take two. She was such a beautiful and warm hearted little girl, that was damaged by the ugly and cold world. You can hear her repeat that age old saying: "Use what you got to get what you want." It's all a front.

She escapes it all through sex, money and drugs; but that innocent little girl just wants a hug. She's still waiting for true love. She hears God calling but she won't look up.

Who Can?

Who can take a heart blackened by fire; soak it in red blood wash it white as snow and make His Seed grow; even though it's been clean from the dirt and mud? - My God.

Who can use my flaws and weaknesses to display His perfect strength, To cover my shortcomings goes to great lengths. - My God

Who can feed me before partaking of my first plate, and I'm still feasting from His goodness, His mercy, and grace? - My God

Who can satisfy a thirsty soul with Living Water, and fill up broken vessels that pour out on the altar? - My God.

Who can give instruction that the wind and water obeys; more radiant than the sun, so the stars gaze? - My God.

Who can hear my whispered prayers like I shouted from the top of my lungs, and when I acted prodigal He still calls me son?- My God.

THE VOICE

THERE IS A VOICE THAT CALLS FROM WITHIN, A PROPELLING FORCE OF VICTORY PROCLAIMING " YOU CAN WIN --- YOU CAN DO IT, DON'T GIVE UP THE FIGHT, TRUST AND BELIEVE THAT ALL WILL BE RIGHT"

COUNTLESS GREAT MEN AND WOMEN HEARD THIS VOICE, AND ACHIEVED MARVELOUS THINGS; EVERY HERO NEEDS A LITTLE WIND BENEATH THEIR WINGS

THIS VOICE WHISPERS WHEN YOU ONLY NEED A NUDGE OR SCREAMS FRANTICALLY WHEN YOU NEED TO BE SHOVED

WHO CAN DENY THAT VOICE WHEN IT SPEAKS SO CLEAR, IT IS THOSE THAT ARE PARALYZED BY FEAR. AFRAID TO MAKE A MOVE EVEN WHEN IT'S THE RIGHT THING TO DO AND YOUR GOAL IS RIGHT THERE IN PLAIN VIEW. IS THIS YOU? ARE YOU AFRAID TO SUCCEED? IS THAT WHY YOU SET GOALS YOU CAN EASILY ACHIEVE? HAVE YOU DENIED THAT VOICE SO LONG THAT YOU DON'T EVEN BELIEVE

I urge you to listen to what the voice is saying and act on it's words without delaying; what you will see is called purpose and what you will feel is called passion. Now is the time for action.

Listen to the voice. It won't steer you astray. Listen to the voice it will guide you all the way. All the way to your destiny; that place of fulfillment and peace, that place where you say "This is where I'm supposed to be"

That voice speaks in every one of us. It is speaking right now. Listen to the voice. Listen to the voice

An unspoken word helps no one

Caution To The Wind

I've weighed the options, counted the cost.
Assessed the likelihood of gains or loss. So now
I'm throwing caution to the wind.

In this faith walk some steps don't make
sense. The idea of leaving a comfort zone
makes me cringe. Fear of the "what ifs" and
"how about"; the inward struggle with
insecurity and doubt.

Double-minded, heart beating triple time. In a
state of paralysis; fear was invoked by
warning signs. Ignoring the fact it
says :"Proceed with caution." Yet I go back to
a place I've been oh so often.

A place of confusion, hopelessness, despair.
The same conditions I prayed to be delivered
from, but at the first sign of resistance; it's
back there that I run. The position that I hate,
but yet I feel safe. Not realizing; that is the
true "danger zone" because the greatest
comfort can be found when you delve into the
unknown.

Pursuing purpose, racing away from the thought of being worthless. I know I have value, I'm truly a treasure. Blessed with gifts that bring riches beyond measure. Something even better than a dollar gained is knowing that growth is impossible without change.

I've always heard be careful, don't do it. You will look like a fool, but it's also foolish to stand still in a cesspool. I understand it takes wisdom to make sound life choices, and one wise move is to limit external voices.

So I get alone with my Creator and seek to find His peace. Once I tune everything else out, I know when He speaks.

I've made mistakes, I've made wrong turns; but through those errors there have been many lessons learned. I've learned to trust my gut, and that voice within. I put my trust in God and throw caution to the wind.

Soliloquies

If you broke down atoms and molecules what you see? God clearly manifested from zero visibility. Revealed soliloquies spoken from infinity through kinetic energy. Before the "Big Bang Theory" or evolution The Spirit hovered the deep. In the beginning was The Word, and The Word still speaks. Through the heat of the sun, the twinkling of the stars and these heavenly bars.

Go back to the drawing board. no theory or query can disprove The Word of The Lord. Before microchips or spaceships from NASA; The Word laid out blue skies and green pastures with white lilies that sprout. So if I kept quiet then the rocks would cry out. Mountains and hills sings songs of praise. Even the trees begin to clap with their hands raised. Pull back the lamp shade. Let your light shine. In this dark world and perilous times.

Peep the signs and wonder how they fall in line with the Word that God in a land before time, and before mankind. I see says the blind, but they are out of their minds because no man has seen God at anytime, but his express image came in the form of Jesus Christ, His Son. The True Light and Righteous One.

The Only Begotten died for the filthy and rotten. Raised the beggar from the dung hill, and lifted up the down trodden. The Lord thy God is One, comprised of The Father, Holy Spirit and Son. It is spoken.

One Soul

God's grace gave me more of what I made waste. He blessed the very thing I made a mess; with my prideful ways, deceitful heart, disobedience to lessons taught. The Master Craftman created beautiful art. From blindness to visions that no man has seen. Once deaf to His Word, but now hears things that are unheard of. It's not what I deserve. It's just His love.

I've been a drunkard, a liar, a thief but He looked past my faults when I got on my knees and asked Christ into my heart. With my mouth I said: "I believe, I believe," like I was there and saw Him bleed. The Blood never loses it's power, and yes it still flows. It's the very same blood that even today saves souls.

Yes. Jesus still saves. He won an eternal battle in just three days. Some ask why I praise? Others ask why I pray? Why I wave my hands when I don't know what to say?

My God is Mighty, Magnificent, He deserves the glory, honor and praise. For the rest of my days, I'll hang the Blood-Stained Banner, and hold a standard. Raising the bar as I press toward the mark. There is a higher call for us all. Seek and save the lost. The Great Commission. That's a great position. We are One Body with One Goal. To not allow the enemy to destroy One Soul.

Christ Hood

A lost soul wandering in the night. Evil spirits lurk in the dark as the blunt sparks. Then his gun cocks; to lick shots at the crackhead that just snatched his rocks. He just re-upped but got caught slippin'. Eyes low; liquor and treed up. In the morning gotta pick his seed up; baby mama trippin' about child support, so now he gotta go to court.

The cash she getting now ain't going to the child. She gets her hair and nails done; buy blunts and Black-n-Milds. She running wild. Hit the clubs hard every weekend. Men in and out creepin' while the kids are sleepin'. No housekeeping. Roaches and bugs on the counter and floor. Don't even have a screen on the screen door.

He's about to break down; he can't take it no more. Where can he turn? He feels like dying, but knows he'll go to Hell and burn. He thought about his grandma. She was always talking about Jesus, and how much he loves us.

Now he's considering church; saying to himself it can't make it no worse. Plus his homeboy since first grade been inviting. He heard God's voice telling him to go but he was fighting. Saying it won't do no good. Is Jesus Christ gonna come save me from the hood?

Does God really care about a thug like me? I heard Pac ask is there a Heaven for a G? I guess I'll see; because I can't live like this. I need a change of pace. Lord I need your grace. It would really be amazin' if it can stop me from blazin' and slangin' dope. Jesus you are my only hope. I need you now. I don't want to live this lifestyle. In and out of jail bouncing from crackhouse to crackhouse. This ain't all good. Again I ask; is Jesus Christ gonna come save me from the hood?

Frustration & Aggravation

Though aggravated and frustrated; I still praised the Lord and the devil hated it. I knew God was in control because I was in the fire but He brought me out pure gold. Shining bright with the garment of praise on. Walking in the Light; shouting and getting my praise on.

Lifting up holy hands and bare feet in the sand. Standing on Holy Ground like Moses. Bush burning as the world keeps turning. Still learning life lessons. Satan testing and stressing yet I kept pressing. Greater is He that is in me. I knew The Truth and that's how I got free. I felt like Peter when he walked on the sea. Lord help me!! Forsook all to follow Christ. Countless hours of studying the Word to divide it right. Day and night.

Pray without ceasing, also hearing so my faith was increasing. Preaching The Word regardless of the season. Telling men to repent, be born again and be not deceived by the doctrine of men. Steadfast in the Gospel and the doctrine of The Apostles.

Even in times when I felt He lead me astray because I ran into obstacles when I do what He said. Like the time I quit my job and my money got tight. My ride broke down and started having problems with my wife. I tried to keep my head up, rejoice in all things but I started to get fed up. Gave up a comfortable life because I heard God so clear, but then started to wonder if I had wax in my ears. He told me to wait; so I waited, but the load got heavy and I became frustrated.

I wanted to help my family but couldn't do nothing. I had to sit back and just watch them struggling. Chalked it up to part of God's will. Can you imagine the war that was going on in my mental battlefield? So I started to do things my way. Having no idea of the price I would have to pay. Loss my joy, loss my peace, loss my hope. Started looking to sinful pleasures to help me cope. Ended up in a fragile state, but thank God for the Holy Ghost that got me back straight, and put me back in formation. When waiting on God endure with patience. Be mindful of frustration and aggravation.

The Press

Back flat, and feet planted. Focused. Raising the bar, pushing with force. Inhale the breath of life, Word of the Lord. Exhale toxic fumes expel it into the void. Pressing with power and perseverance. Endurance from God's Spirit. Running the course that was laid. Obtain maximum gains through patience and faith. Stamina builds up the inner man, converting the sinner man. Through spiritual disciplines, and meal plan. Chew the Scriptures, drink Living Water. Partake of the Fruit of the Spirit, and Bread of the Altar. Spend time in prayer to tighten the core, Obedience can stretch and sometimes make the muscles sore. When God speaks to the cardio, it's inaudible but still loud and clear. Wraps His words in love to cast out all fears. So the next step, will be the best step. So stick to the routine, and get in all the reps.

When God Cries

With every wrong turn made or hard bed laid - God cries
He sheds a tear when a child shortens their years.
Dishonoring the ones that brought them here.

When a woman is between the sheets with a man that's not
her own; knowing he has a wife at home. The man that lays
with the wife of another, the ones on the down low, in the
closet or under cover. Choosy lovers gambling with their
soul; fulfilling dark passions with no regard for the
recompense of their actions. God cries.

How can you dismiss a God that see all? As He sits high
and looks low; the tears flow because He loves the world
so. So much He sent His Only Begotten for all to be
redeemed. A love that ears haven't heard and eyes haven't
seen. So they ask; "What manner of love is this?" - While
God cries

He watches with teary eyes because of the world's sin, and
all He wants to do is be a friend. A very present help in the
time of need. A provider, a protector, a Father, a guide.
One that will never leave, forsake or deny. God cries

Yes He cries for every dream aborted, and vision distorted.
Each time his child believes a lie; this is His reply: "Why
can't they just trust Me? I desire to see them prosper and
grow, but they just won't let go and hold on to Me. I'm able
to keep them from falling and give them rest. I see that
they are weary, wounded and weak. I weep because they
won't have faith in Me." - This is what it sounds like
"When God Cries."

The Secret Place

Abiding in the Secret Place I find peace. I find refuge and strength. I'm safe because The Lord is my fortress and impenetrable shield. He's my rock and sword on the battlefield.

When I kneel and pray. I'm assured He'll lead the way. His paths lead to life, to purpose, an destiny. Time in the Secret Place brings out the best in me. Why stress the enemy that's testing me? I set my affections on the God that protects me, and continually blesses me. It's His plans that will manifest in me.

No weapon formed against me shall prosper or prevail, I WILL NOT FAIL, I WILL SUCCEED. Why? - Because My God shall supply all my need. According to His riches, not my bank account. I'm abundantly supplied with unlimited amounts.

Every assignment, every dream, every vision... If it is birthed from God, He has made provision. I walk in confidence, boldness and victory. I proclaim it with a shout, and continually lift up His name with my mouth.

He is El Shaddai, all sufficient, and more than enough. He makes the crooked places straight and smoothes out the roads that are rough.

I press into the Secret Place of my God and draw nigh, such a humbling experience to be in the presence of the Most High.

Many fall at my right hand, by my side, but the enemy can't come near. No evil thing, plague or calamity is welcome here.

He even sends His angels to walk with me in case I stumble, and that let's me know He's a very present help in a time of trouble. And because I seek His face; He shows me His hand. Due to my willingness to obey; I eat the good of the land. So why should I stray from a perfect plan and follow the Devil's scheme? Know he's tempting me to abandon my faith and destroy my hopes and dreams.

I dwell in that Secret Place. Hidden in Christ where I can't be seen. While my God fights the battle against the enemy and his regime. In the shadow of the Almighty and under His wing. My heart sings because time in the Secret Place brings open rewards, and my life brings glory to the name of The Lord... When I dwell in the Secret Place.

XXX

Up in the late night; engaged in a spiritual fight. Better yet a war; waited to late to pull my sword. The enemy had me trapped off I missed my escape route.

I should have turned the TV off. Shouldn't have had it on at all because I saw some things that was appealing to my flesh. It wasn't KFC but all I saw was thighs and breasts. Then a website flashed across the screen. My wife is snoring in her sleep. I hope she's having sweet dreams.

So I jump up and even though I know it ain't right. I'm surfing the internet looking for XXX-rated sites. Trying to creep and make sure my wife stays asleep; even locking the room door. Surfing until three and four in the morning; didn't heed the Holy Ghost warning. I know I need to repent but I don't feel sorrow, and thinking what if Christ come back tomorrow.

There was an indwelling sin that kept causing me to fall, attacking my mind at times that I'm walking tall. It's like I can't stop sinning. Can't stop lusting even though I say I'm trusting in my Lord and Savior Jesus Christ.

Even though I love my neighbors and try to live right but while striving for perfection at times I chose the wrong direction. At the intersection contemplating Christ lessons;

But then made a move according to the flesh. That's why I have to die daily; repent and resurrect. Turned from death, and chose life abundantly. Now I'm back on the path of my destiny. I'm set free.

Verbal Assualt

Roll up with the Most High God, pullin' your card. Like Chris Brown when we "Stomping The Yard".With no suits, just jeans and Timberland boots. Strapped with the Word of Truth, ready to shoot. My finger on the trigger, ready to squeeze. Creep up on 'em in the spot while they're blazing trees.

Burst like gamma rays when the verbal A-K sprays. Rapid fire with the King James. When it's time for the showdown, I let off the whole round. Got the whole squad shook, and petrified in the background. Went from laughter to "Tears of a Clown." Where do you stand when your world is turned upside-down?

Your sin before your face, feeling disgraced because you dissed grace and have to see God face to face. But y'all don't want see eye-to-eye. Caught eating the Devil's lie instead of Shepherd's Pie. Ain't no alibis when it's Judgement Day. And you can't say He didn't try to show you The Way.

Thought you was bullet-proof until you was blasted with The Truth. The Holy Ghost pricked your heart with infallible proofs.

Tried to bust back but your aim was off.
Tried to swing, but you missed because your arms
were too short. Can't box with God
even though your head is hard. He'll split your
wig then heals your scars. He'll give it to you raw.
He can sautee or grill it in a pan or a skillet.
Maybe pour on some hot sauce to make sure that
you feel it.

He made me a soldier with stripes in the army of
The Lord. Nice with the hands and skilled with
The Sword. Strong in the spirit so I flex like Ford.
In the middle of the streets shouting Jesus is
Lord. He can crush into powder the ones that try
to be hard.

Too late to repent once He cracks the sky. He'll be
back before the flash hit you're twinkling eye.
Too late to say wait, It will be already over, can't
fix your face or shake yourself sober. Every
tongue must confess and every knee must bow.
So you might as well go and do it right now.

S.O.S.

Fist tightly clinched, pressed against my chest. Thoughts as of rushing waters pound upon the shores of my intellect. All of my being baptized into uncertainty, submerged in the sea of doubt. A pool of wantonness.

Drifting towards the horizon. However it also drifts. The further I float, It becomes more distant. So here I am; backstroking against the current. As I drive myself toward the deep-end. I ask myself; How is it that I feel so shallow? I struggle to make it back ashore but the riptides of life draw me further out to sea. The sands of the shore disappear; leaving me in dismay and scared.

I then plunge into an abyss of gloominess and dejection. A Great Depression. Ships pass in the night. However I see no light. Not a flicker or a flare. Only fear as the temperature drops to near freezing point.

I LONG FOR WARMTH AND SECURITY; NEITHER IS NEAR. I NEED A LIFE JACKET. I CAN NO LONGER STAY AFLOAT. MY HOPE IS DROWNING. I GASP FOR AIR, BUT MY LUNGS ARE FLOODED WITH DESPAIR.

I'M SINKING... DOWN I GO; I QUICKLY SENT OUT AND S.O.S. TO THE SAVIOR OF SOULS. IT WAS IN THAT INSTANCE I BEGAN TO SEE THAT THERE WAS A LIGHT FROM THE LIGHTHOUSE; SHINING ON ME.

I GRABBED THE SAVIORS HAND. HE LED ME BACK TO PEACEFUL SHORES. NO LONGER IS MY SOUL ALARMED; I AM SAFE AND SECURE. NO LONGER SINKING, AFRAID OR COLD. I'M ABIDING IN JESUS. THE SAVIOR OF SOULS.

BlackBreaking

Back breaking, soul aching, dignity taking
Black Mother raping. Black Son killing, riotous
villains. Chameleons. Bending and twisting.
Scriptures missing from the heart of
Christians

Sharp contradictions in their non-fictions.
Tension and friction build mental prisons
and cause spiritual incisions. One way ticket
to Hell first class. Getting nowhere fast. Hope
you enjoy the ride. Got my traveling shoes on,
but their untied so can't wade in the water.

Dumb like a sheep to the slaughter.
Inheritance of ignorance to sons and
daughters. No respect for mothers and
fathers. How is it that we're going down hill
but yet it's getting harder. Call me a social
martyr, when I do things decent and in order.
Help us Father. That's the cry of your people.
But do those prayers go past the church
steeple?

They say I was created equal. Well when did I become less? Is it the color of my flesh or my righteousness. The truth shall manifest and expose the works of the dark. Speak the issues of life and reveal the condition of the heart.

Propaganda and slander influence us all back to the mindset of Neanderthals, but not I. I'm a child of the Most High. That's why I stay fly. So fresh and so clean. Speak divine wisdom through prophetic dreams. Ahead with full steam, call me hot head. By the way The "N" Word is not dead.

It's alive and well. As real as the flames in Hell for those that rebel against the Truth of the Gospel. The deity of Christ and the ways of the Apostles. Not the Christ in your picture frame, but the one that heals the sick and upholds the lame. He's the name above all names and the King of Kings not James.

Beat By The Drum

There was a kick, then hi-hat and just like that; caught by the snare. I'm floored that any Tom, Dick and Harry that can carry a tune send so many crashing to their doom. Like cymbals; they use symbols and flash signs. Tones and frequencies that control the mind, all by design. Evil spirits riding the bass lines while the young kids bump and grind due to vibrations sent up and down their spines. In the meantime, The Devil's on the mixing board; turning knobs and pushing faders. You see He's a Pro at using these Tools to make them look like fools.

Well crafted chords make them forget about their Lord. He conveys his evil message through chants and metaphors. Make you groove to a Auto-Tune that leaves the mind chopped and screwed, misconstrued; because they don't understand what comes after the interlude. Plucking on the heart strings. Picking and grinning because he's winning as long as he can keep them sinning, and pretending they are amongst the stars.

In actuality they are trapped behind hooks and bars; about sex and cars, drugs and street wars. Not seeing that it's all fiction. The groove is like an addiction. You press pause, but it plays on. Over and over in your mind like rewind, but it's fast-forward at a tempo that you can't control. He then pops the big question: "How much for your soul?"

Let's check the record. Let's make a deal. Why not put a label on what we have? Something deeper than fun and games. Something deeper than the laughs. I can make you hot. Don't look at it like a contract. It's just a reference or a point of contact. Before you know it. The dream becomes a nightmare because all they heard a kick, and a hi-hat so got caught by the snare.... You just got beat by the drum.

The Master's Peace

I'm not what many would call a masterpiece, but I'm The Master's Piece. In my fallen state; He called me outstanding. I was on a winding road racing with reckless abandon, but He taught me to stay in my lane. I rest in The Master's Peace.

That peace that passes all understanding. That peace that softens the blow of a crash landing. Face first on the runway; I wanted to run away; but peace said "stay." I can smooth out the rough spots and make your crooked paths straight. I decided to rest in The Master's Peace.

I was afflicted, dejected, mocked and rejected; but peace said "you are accepted." No morals, convictions and bound to addictions; but peace said "you are forgiven." I rest in The Master's Peace

Through trial and error. Many trials, many errors; I learned to stand upright by leaning on The Everlasting Arms. I stand on the rooftops and shout that He's a shelter in the time of storm. I rest in The Master's Peace

My value exceeds what is seen by the naked eye. Don't be confounded by what you see. I am fearfully and wonderfully made. I am a masterpiece. Safe in My Father's arms. I rest in The Master's Peace.

Love Is...

Love looks over and overlooks faults. Love is flawless

Love pays the cost of things that can't be bought. Love is priceless

Love understands that it will never be over. Love is forever

To be drunk in love; one would have to be sober. Love is intoxicating.

Love sees potential when there is no vision. Love is blind.

Love is the helping hand when there is no provision. Love will make a way

Love is the roadmap when there is no direction. Love is the guide

Love is a covering when there is no protection. Love is a shield

Love is a shelter when there is no roof. Love is a dwelling place

Love is absolute even if there is no proof. Love is God

Open The Door

You already have the keys. Why are you waiting?
t's not locked, yet you stand there and won't even
knock. - Open the Door

You've had glimpses of what's on the other side yet
you are just standing there. Time on the clock goes
tick...tock. - Open the Door

Are you afraid of letting go what's on this side? Are
there some things you are trying to hide? Is that why
you won't? - Open the Door.

Everything you need and more will be available if you
just..- Open the Door.

Standing in front of the door is so many metaphors. It
can represent old scars and open sores. It can
represent past mistakes, failures and heartbreaks.
Misunderstandings and improper planning;
disappointments, rejection, over-protection.
weakness,insecurity, jealousy, envy, vulnerability or
just being plain silly.

But when you open The Door; you find what God has
in store. Comfort, healing, counsel and leading.
Dreams, visions, purpose and ambition. Love, joy,
peace and blessing. Acceptance, protection, a new
direction. Will you please just... Open the Door.

www.ingramcontent.com/pod-product-compliance
Lightning Source LLC
Chambersburg PA
CBHW031530040426
42445CB00009B/468